My Trip to Yellowstone

by Carol Pugliano

Yellowstone is in three states.

My family and I went to Yellowstone National Park. Yellowstone is our country's first national park. This is what we saw there.

This fountain is called Old Faithful.

This looks like a big water fountain! The water shoots up in the air many times a day.

This waterfall is very tall.

(l)Scenics of America/PhotoLink/Getty Images, (r)Adam Jones/Digital Vision/Getty Images

What goes up and down in Yellowstone? Water! We saw many waterfalls in the park. This one is 308 feet high!

The rocks are full of color.

This is a hot spring.
The water gets very hot
under the ground. Then it
lets off steam.

This forest has trees made of stone.

Long ago, dirt and ash covered many trees. Over time, the trees turned to stone!

Yellowstone is like a huge zoo! But there are no cages. Many animals roam free in the park. We saw bison, wolves, moose, and bears.

There are many deer in Yellowstone.

Yellowstone is a beautiful
place. I am glad it is
a park that everyone
can visit!

Yellowstone!

Tell your partner what you learned about Yellowstone National Park. Ask what your partner learned.

 ## Go See It!

Draw a picture of something you would like to see at Yellowstone. Write a sentence. *I want to see the _____ at Yellowstone.*

My USA

GR G • Benchmark 12 • Lexile 370

Grade K • Unit 8 Week 2

www.mheonline.com

The **McGraw·Hill** Companies

ISBN-13 978-0-02-119487-2
MHID 0-02-119487-4

9 780021 194872

EAN

99701

K

McGraw Hill **Education**